SMOKING THE BIBLE

Also by Chris Abani

Poetry

Sanctificum
There Are No Names for Red
Feed Me the Sun
Hands Washing Water
Dog Woman
Daphne's Lot
Kalakuta Republic

Fiction

The Secret History of Las Vegas
Song for Night
The Virgin of Flames
Becoming Abigail
Graceland
Masters of the Board

Memoir

The Face

SMOKING THE BIBLE
CHRIS ABANI ⋮ *Poems*

COPPER CANYON PRESS
PORT TOWNSEND, WASHINGTON

Cover art: Patrick Alston, *Lack Thereof*. Acrylic, oil, and ink on
sewn canvas, linen, and fabric.

Copper Canyon Press is in residence at Fort Worden State Park
in Port Townsend, Washington, under the auspices of Centrum.
Centrum is a gathering place for artists and creative thinkers from
around the world, students of all ages and backgrounds, and
audiences seeking extraordinary cultural enrichment.

LIBRARY OF CONGRESS
CATALOGING-IN-PUBLICATION DATA
Names: Abani, Chris, author.
Title: Smoking the Bible : poems / Chris Abani.
Description: Port Townsend, Washington : Copper Canyon Press, 2022. |
    Summary: "A collection of poems by Chris Abani"—Provided by
publisher.
Identifiers: LCCN 2021053292 (print) | LCCN 2021053293 (ebook) |
ISBN 9781556596285 (paperback) | ISBN 9781619322547 (epub)
Subjects: LCGFT: Poetry.
Classification: LCC PR9387.9.A23 S64 2022 (print) | LCC
PR9387.9.A23 (ebook) | DDC 821/.914—dc23/eng/20211029
LC record available at https://lccn.loc.gov/2021053292
LC ebook record available at https://lccn.loc.gov/2021053293

9 8 7 6 5 4 3 2 FIRST PRINTING

COPPER CANYON PRESS
Post Office Box 271
Port Townsend, Washington 98368
www.coppercanyonpress.org

Acknowledgments

Thanking Sarah Tolan Mee, who makes it all possible—life and art—my best friend.

Thanking Aikulola Rose Abani—there are no words for the awe of you.

Thanking my friends and readers: Kwame Dawes, Matthew Shenoda, Joseph Millar, and Aracelis Girmay.

Thanking Michael Wiegers—editor and friend.
And the crew at Copper Canyon Press—also fam.

Thanks to *WLT*, *PSA*, *Papercuts*, and other journals that published iterations of these poems.

And my family: essential, primordial, and love.

If I forgot to mention anyone—mea culpa; aging brain is a motherfucker.

for Gregory and Aikulola

For darkness restores what light cannot repair.

Contents

SMOKING THE BIBLE

Flay

The point of a pen opens a hole
into a soul's dereliction. This search

for the right word bores through stone.
Sunlight takes no measure of what is clung to.

A man can place the half-dome
of a tomato, slice into flesh,

and cut an island of loss. Migrant,
punished by spice and the scent of cooking,

you wake up on a cold day in another country
and put your faith in hot rice and braised goat,

and the persistent aftertaste of a lost home.
Gospels are made of less than this.

But outside it is morning. A summer breeze
burns down to the water and the ocean begins.

Quest

When the doctor said *Terminal*,
you went silent, and I set off, Brother. *Journey*
is a word trembling at a platform's edge.
Traveling as a way of emptying out all
that cannot be emptied.
Only to arrive back
at myself twice as full but with a shovel, blade
worn to nub from the digging. There
will be a reckoning, but I promise
to walk with you as far as I can
in this fragile light buoyant with loss.

Nostalgia

A train travels through a Midwestern cornfield,
yellow slants to gold as the sun leans heavy on the horizon;

this meager harvest of memory and hope—
the entropy of a coffee cup half spilling into

a wash of half-truths. A sweet decline.
To have spent your life thinking, I am

the good one, the stable one, then one
morning in a city between the city you call

home and the one you are traveling to, you
accept: you are migrant. This is where you

find yourself, somewhere between coercion
and insubstantial desire, the slow decomposition that is

life. Yet for now this half-light, the gentle
sway on the tracks, music enough for this journey.

BIRTH RIGHT

Thin pages brittle with words and
two brothers, one elder. The biblical,
unavoidable here. And there is the rub.
To come to self, to skin, is to rip away another, separate,
tear. Train snaking track, snaking thoughts—
window as page, margin as frame, what is kept within,
what slips away. From beyond the willow's lazy bow
into river, beyond the crane stabbing for minnows
in the shallows, beyond the reflected sunlight,
in a cathedral the tints of stained glass,
that addendum to light
that tempers it to grace.

Sojourn

The train bores through corn like a weevil.
Birds hop across drooping leaves like scribes.

An immigrant, I try to read origin here but cannot.
Mighty nations erased in all but place-names,

reduced to fit the small malice of a conqueror's heart.
What will not yield to the poet's gaze will be overwritten.

Sure as ink rides the sway of paper.
But there, in a tear in the green and yellow,

a red tractor idles like a slow-burning coal.
Fire, that man burning on TV,

skin melting, somewhere between Africa and Lampedusa.
Flaming in the prow of a boat.

You turn from the image, say: *Death will find you
how it wills, and as it wills.* The chemo in you is

fire too. And in the end,
in someone's heart, we too must burn.

Excavation

> for David Doris

The fecund smell of loam, rotting wood, mushroom, and beets.
Other things also—earthworms at their workings.
They eat and excrete every grain of earth.
An eternity of sustenance and renewal, a world reformed.
Brother, our love is an endless summer turned over and over,
and yet so much is still this—
that we are deformed early, the pattern set:
curry still smells good, rhubarb baked in a pie,
tea heavy with milk and sugar reminds us that failure is
sated only for that moment, mitigated for a while between
the aroma of preparation and the last scrape of the fork.

Light Flame, Turn Rebel

I remember your first blaze, carpet of flame
spreading with ease through a valley of corn.
The dry cobs awaiting the farmer's hands
to pluck and smooth them.
The dry resistance of kernels ground
to submission on a worn stone. Or planted,
yellowed teeth turning to seed.

What flared in you, ignited a match
cupped from the wind and held to stalk?
Did your hands tremble in the moment?
Your immolation as boy, your incarnation as rebel?

And what did Father see in that barren blackness
punctuated by still-smoking stalks?
Your plea or the blackening of his heart?
The scar of a farm burned to the ground?
Even this devastation can grow love.

Cameo: Broach

Outside, snow travels in unhurried drifts.
Inside the overheated train, fog shrouds
the dirty window, drawing mottled patterns.
A second landscape of impermanence and breath.
With a finger, I trace a cameo not unlike
the broaches Mother wore high on the neck.
You were always her favorite. The best of us.
How to broach influence? How to speak of us
without speaking of Father and Mother?
A swath of light falls across the tray table,
an ant trembles under the weight of the bright.
I fold an origami bird, think of hand-rolled
cigarettes made from Bible pages,
suddenly given flight by flame, egrets
immolated in the burn.

WHITE EGRET

The whole earth is filled with the love of God.
                                KWAME DAWES

A stream in a forest and a boy fishing,
heart aflame, head hush, tasting the world—
lick and pant. The Holy Scripture
is animal not book.
I should know, I have smoked
the soul of God, psalm burning
between fingers on an African afternoon.
And how is it that death can open up
an alleluia from the core of a man?
How easily the profound fritters away in words.
And the simple wisdom of my brother:
What you taste with abandon
even God cannot take from you.
All my life, men with blackened insides
have fought to keep
the flutter of a white egret in my chest
from bursting into flight, into glory.

Cameo: Cremation

Smoke and ash portended loss the night
Mother fed her diary into flame,
sheet by sheet, line by cursive line,
and then a wind wove through, enough
to blow flame back, searing skin.
She hesitated a moment, penitent, then pulled back.
She let it hurt for one second too long: for regret,
or for the sweet torture of fire? Sometimes
you just burn your life and begin again.
And even again. A single blister
rose on her hand, the size of a baby's heart.

THREAD

A small gutter in front of a wood-and-tin shack.
Inside a woman and a sewing machine chatter
in repair of things that can never be gathered again.
For a forced migration, even Atlantic, even Mediterranean.
For a flight from a definite death.
For a woman drowning to save her child.
For slavery, the new heavy with the grit of desert.
For slavery, the old heavy with salt water.
For a boat furrowing ocean to plowed field.
To make full restitution is an impossible dream.
The final measure of a body's desperation
hums to buoyancy, to wish, not to the fact of ruin.
The red earth of my homeland is both wound and suture.
Nomad is the human urge: fear is the need to stay.
Word is what says, *Not even one of us will be forgotten.*

Glow

There was a fire in you, a delight
in tasting the world, touch,
lick, roll, tweeze, pinch, smoke—
but that flicker of light was a burn too much
for Father and he made himself your fireman.
He called it love, I think, when alone inside his head.
Compassion, even. And how the world
and everyone hurts us for our own good.
How a fist weaves to tender touch,
the cut cane a mamba's strike.
And each bite of cane to flesh,
this thing he tried to extinguish grew more tensile.
You would watch him prowl the yard, alert like a goat.
I read the world to you—said: *There are plums in Italy*
so plump they are called nun's thighs.
And you drank it in, beauty and irreverence.
Then I went away to seminary and solitude.
Church and the smell of incense remind me we stole
communion wafers for breakfast
in a mud-walled chapel perched
on the edge of a cliff,
lit only by flickering candles.

Presence and Aftermath

The way a photograph burns like a heart closing
in on itself. An enfolding of ash and color.
Words more fragile than morning light,
more realistic and meaningful than *heal.*
There are softer words for a beginning
than *vengeance* or *forgiveness,* even *restoration.*
An erect spine is also the refusal over a life-
time of the many things given and taken.
The detritus of death and the body.
Duty doesn't always supersede love and anger.
There is always more that keeps a son
from his father's funeral—presence and aftermath.

POET DESPERATE FOR SONG

A boy in a park brandished a knife
to gut me. You rose halfway, skinny
sweet boy tensed into an upright cobra,
said in a voice close to a hiss, *I'm ready.*
Struck him in the face, licked his blood
from your knuckles, your head cocked to one side.
Now cancer guts you; head cocked
to one side, you say, *I'm ready.*
Outside a cardinal lands on a branch
meaning God, meaning ancestor,
meaning the heart of Mercy.

MANHOOD

And that uncle, with a look of regret
for what was to come, sang softly, *Jujuwua.*
The shuddering moan of blood,
a song to calm the sacrificial,
the loss across the river.
The way a dying animal will look at you
is seared into me.
We die together and all over again.
And the snaking cane he brought down,
like Baal's priests, drew blood,
the prayer is the pause between each lash,
that breathily sung word: *Jujuwua.*
You were Elijah gone to heaven to fetch a fire,
but what of the witness who cannot turn away?

QUESTION

What a short rope the larynx is,
the hanged man, sacrifice as sin.
And how many hung from trees
for redemption, for clarity, for fear?
What is this insatiable murder of trees?

In Atlanta I read under a Mamie poster.
And later a white man asked me
why there was so much violence in my novel.
And I was unsure whether he meant:
I'm sorry for all the violence we have done to you.

Outside my B&B room, an old oak from which,
the white owner told me with no irony,
black bodies were hanged.
But I too stand on the path of privilege.
Why as an African haven't I asked
how many people my people
put on the road to enslavement?

THAT EARLY SUNDAY

Morning light, skittish, a dove on the verge of startle
falls in a thin red line through muted glass,
resolutely cutting the edge of the altar steps in half.
Through an open window sun and shadow pattern
the Madonna with the sad eyes and that odd red-lipped smirk.
Too early for the congregation, too early even for the priest.
Alone in the damp whitewashed chapel, two brothers prepare.
Swinging the censer, hot coals smoldering, crackling as
frankincense calls an angelic host in a sickly sweetness.

We polish the benches by sliding khaki-clad butts
down the pews, reckless, afraid of neither God nor splinters.
As the blue of early dawn eases into the rose blush of sunrise,
we shuffle into the sacristy, prepare the priest's robes,
alb, chasuble, stole, laid on the wooden table, an order of fabric.
We shrug into surplice and cope, robe and short cape, white and red,
the blood and the sanctified, the innocent and the bloodied.
Shoving handfuls of stale communion wafers into our mouths,
we break fast on holy water and the body of Christ.

Years later you ask me whether that priest ever did damage
beyond his whiskey-heavy insults and wild fists.
In your eyes, there was acceptance; if murder need be done—
But the priest is long dead and besides, I say, we escaped
the worst of those days. We both remember the morning
I knocked the censer over and lit my robes on fire
and you calmly emptied holy water over me. Amen.

The Ghost Speaks

Here things unknown are spoken with ease.
The dead hummingbird on my mother's grave
cannot be explained, nor that way in which
love is a kind of humiliation. The journey to the chapel
on the hill through an early morning mist and silence
as empty as a priest's heart.

You tear Psalm 23 from Father's leather-bound Bible,
roll it. Silently I recite, *The Lord is my shepherd; I shall not*—
You consider the scroll and with the match and flame
already licking the edge of the paper, you ask if I think
God remembers my name.

I feel an immensity open
in my chest, and say it doesn't matter,
it's easy to usurp an angel's name. But deep
inside me the great migration begins, the steady trek
to adolescence and beyond, and the knowledge
that no light can be trusted entirely.
Not even the flame of a psalm inhaled by a river.

A Small Awe

The afternoon feels like a vast distance,
a sky heavy with rain clouds.
The day is like a flickering screen
and what it illumines slips quickly to shadow.
How age diminishes childhood to a fading stain
on a tablecloth; okra stew from a lunch served
by the constrained heart of a mother longing for more.
How Giacometti's tortured bodies carry a redemption,
always alluding to the Christ on the cross, perhaps.
Or maybe just the simple unadorned body of pain
marking a human crossing the desert of life.
Reason always ends at the edge of water—
ocean, lake, river, even a pond.
The world we carry inside follows us everywhere.
Our imagined home remains nostalgia: shiver,
ache, loss, and also a flutter of release.
How pigeons lift in a cloud of frenzy,
then settle back to the duty of crumbs.

GRACE

A boy we played with as children.
A boy who never pushed anyone in soccer.
A boy who struggled to kill chickens for dinner.
That boy, grown to man, sharpened a machete
all the while chatting to his father who lazily
shelled and ate peanuts in the veranda's shade.

Getting up from the whetstone, testing
the edge of the knife on his thumb,
he climbed the three steps to his father and
let loose his anger with one cut.
He smiled, it was rumored, smiled and kissed
the top of his father's head before walking off.

The peanuts frothed through his father's throat
but such was the lineage of that anger that
the old man in his seventies walked to hail a cab
only to die in the ER when they pried his hand
away from the bloody gash of his throat.

I want to make a poem of this, Brother,
I want to make a song of love—
That boy, our cousin, that boy but for
the perverted beauty of grace,
that boy was you, that boy was me.

And still our father died alone,
which is its own kind of anger,
its own revenge. And one can wake up
halfway around the world when
a parent dies on the other side.
Wake up in a sweat-drenched panic
at the very cusp of crossing.

There are many euphemisms for
death and dying in English, but not Igbo.
For us the moment is singular.
Death comes. Death takes.
Do you remember all the boys
in you that were that boy?
All the hate in you that died so
you would not wet a stone grab a blade
and hone your anger to a fine edge?
You must do, you must do
and I know because I have
seen your fierce love for your children.
Seen the bees you keep in your small English
garden—hate that has died to honey.

Ritual Is Journey

And suddenly it's raining, streaking train windows.
And light becomes a bird, a particular flutter.
What shadows let slip, tattoo patterns on skin,
repairs with needle and ink,
and the whisper of lineage.
To be a man, to be black, to be a black man,
is a dangerous journey. My heart is a knot
burling a staff, wisdom won blow by blow.
Father, I say, Father.
Mercy. Come, mercy, come.
Brother, we share genes so old
England was still black, and Africa
was the only present tense in the world.
As we unzip tracks in flashes of light,
I seek an impossible dream.
Yet all rivers flow to the ocean.
All the doors white men
closed in my father's face
cannot compare to the void
in which my mother found no door.
Mercy. Come, mercy, come.
This is no lament; women deserve our awe.
In Africa we say, *He who strikes a woman strikes stone.*
If women called out from all their loss
and in all their power, blood would drown everything.
And does that first black woman regret letting us live?
Still, ritual is journey, atonement is real.
As you lay dying, I asked, *What is your biggest regret?*
Every kindness withheld, you said.
Every flicker of pleasure denied, you said.
Look, you said, *sunlight.*

Olokun

Into the inky smoke of lake mist, Evanston's
lighthouse throws a weak fire, more gleam than flame,
but sufficient light for ghosts
to winter by, and so I stand on the empty beach.
In my hand a plastic tub of cut fruit, meager
offering for any sea god though this is what I bring.
This and the oblong of kola nut, flesh of my flesh,
flesh of my lineage, the tart communication of augury.

I've been here before, in morning's lazy yawn,
noon's bright parade and the purple honey
of summer sunset; but fall nights hold purpose.
So I'm here, O ancient god of my people.
The ghosts watch me with silent expectation.
Make your move, man. Wield your blessed craft.

I bend to empty fruit into the hungry lap,
thinking of a blind carpenter in my father's village
who could lean into the straight furrow
of plane and wood, shave a curl
delicate, ebony turned gossamer,
a hard stroke turned prayer,
each shaving falling in
a dialect too pure for paper.

Surf licks the last piece of fruit and I break
kola into a diviner's spread, *Ase, baba, ase.*
My ghosts smile, almost imperceptible in the dark,
turn and fall back into the swell
and now there is only the hiss of wave, the pale fire
of lighthouse on the water's crest.

Offertory

You can smell a humid rain miles before the water
envelopes you, a hot smell, ripe as a swamp.
This is the day, you say, the cusp of return, restitution for sin.
The animal is calm under your hand, but still a throb of life.
To measure the distance a knife travels
in wonder toward the neck,
or something like fear, or regret, or even, say, delight.
In the shade of the shrine, your lineage
ghosts between light and shade.
Though we know grief cannot raise the dead,
we speak the spells nonetheless.
Nothing outlasts the arc of the heart.
No intelligence can reason away sorrow.
Still, gin cupped in prayer is a fragile gift.
We speak in libation to remember.

HORSES

You astride a brown horse, naked
torso painted white and red with clay,
so free, so wild. It made you sad
when that magnificence breathing against your leg
was offered to the dead.

I called you from a favela in Rio to tell you
of the white horse I saw in the fast gloom
of dusk running on an island of green
in the stink of brown sewage water.
Told you of the boy with the fresh bullet hole
in his chest, guarding that regal ripple of muscle.
Told you he explained that this beauty too
couldn't last, it would die for need, for food.

You called me a romantic fool, suckered by hope
for a future where our grief is set free,
hundreds of wild mustangs racing across a butte.
You said, *Find a steady woman and in the grace
of quotidian domesticity, raise children
whose hearts are wild horses no one can trap.
Or God,* you said. Like that light, the freedom
of the eagle we saw lift off an unsteady palm tree,
or that horse in a favela bolting for a dying light.

INSOMNIA

And you, Brother? Do you roam the night, too?
See ghosts, or your child's discarded toy?
To slip through a sleepless house
fetid as breath from a spice-heavy dinner.
A small leather-bound book of psalms
in Hebrew and English, handmade pages
facing the wrong way like a life lived in regret.
In that hush, I break Jerusalem into voice.
Prayer as relentless as the grit of sand in a shoe.
This meditation is at once romance and sorrow,
a stutter, a life fallen short. In the yard, rabbits
track an insistent alphabet across pristine snow.
The sky hollowed out by stars.

Rain

Why were you beaten each time?
For running away or for coming back?
Your gaunt and funky body was evidence enough
you had been punished already. And like Pilate
I hand you over to that mob of angry men—
Father and his brothers—head down, unable to stand
before the fear in your eyes, a feral beast.
You touch my face in forgiveness and
I burn with a thing I still have no name for.

In the warm shower your body welted from caning,
the blood, rust-orange, runs down your leg,
the left one, cocked against the sting,
you ask me to soap your back and I understand
that you need to be touched tenderly
after our father's violence.
Even such a thing can bind brothers.

I stand by French doors looking through the rain
into the strange luminosity of a Nigerian
cement bathroom mottled by green moss,
the brown leak of rusty pipes, to that slender
boy with long hair and light skin
shadowed by pain

a man approaches a door
and steps through.

How to Write a Love Letter to Your Brother

A train station silent but for the hum of tracks.
An all-night diner in the shadows,
parking lot all but deserted. Places I found you
when you ran away from home.
The in-between places souls like us haunt,
caught in an impossible melancholy,
its own sweet addiction.

I want to say I love you to all the men
our father couldn't be, all the men
our brothers are trying to be, and the man
you are—a creature iridescent yet wrong for it.
I want to say I'm sorry, I wanted to save you.

When I fetched you, Brother, I fetched you for love.
For the sweat of sincere rosaries, a hope of beads.
For Mother's pleading, her red-eyed worry.
For all the ways one cannot speak
of an unbearable light, a sky burning,
smoke choking birds in flight.

When Father stepped to you, just before
the first blow landed, I heard you
begging, negotiating, pleading.
What began as words became a keening.

ALLEGORY

Boys pine for the gravel of a father's touch.
This desire is a jackal scavenging
all that is good in our lives.
Picking flesh from bone, bloom from stalk,
water from valley, until a terrible drought
drives us from our hearts
into a world of flame and search.
Father beat me with a branch from a palm tree.
Incensed I went to my uncle,
the native priest, to put a hex on him.
To bring him to ruin. To bring him
to his knees before me.
The old priest smiled and said, *First go and cut*
forty branches. Anger made the task easy.
He taught me to trim the leaves
from the branch and the spines
from the leaves, and the grip to hold
a handful, slip a knot of reeds and tie.
Passing it he said, *Go, sweep*
the anger from your heart.

LINEAGE

Someone has always wanted my skin.
For the Egu it was the genocide of Aro.
For the Aro it was the devastation of the British.
For the British it was my father's quiet revenge,
blow after blow dealt to my mother,
his white English wife—
rupture and repair, scar and keloid.
My skin is the voice of my ancestors
sounding in the well of a drum.
My skin is a cloak, sacred
painted spells. I have released
the anger inside me,
a bird flying across oceans,
dying a thousand deaths but never dead.
My body is the house of tomorrow.
My skin is prophecy.

Snake

When that guard-post sergeant pulled us up,
Father drunk, Mother in a silver lamé dress,
    Where to?
Innocuous but for the sneer, the leering teeth.
You covered my eyes with sweaty palms, fingers gapped,
a venetian at half-mast. I see the bend at the waist
to look into the window, the way his eyes linger on Mother.
    Home.
Father doesn't so much answer as bark.
The sergeant bristles, says,
    Step out.
Your fingers close together and I am blind as I hear
Father's belt unbuckle. In the silence
I imagine him bent over, trousers by his ankles, for the search.
But there is something else in that dark silence
wet with the sweat of a boy's palms,
something like a dog's tongue.
I see it even now, the belt dangling from Father's hand,
licking at the road, coiling
like a mamba ready to strike.
We are no strangers to death and I can see
the bolt of the rusty rifle pull back
before its throaty rasp. Then
the passenger door opens. I hear the imperial
delight of Mother's best English accent.
    Officer, would you like a cigarette?
The pause is heavy with humidity, heavy with posture.
The bolt eases back home gently and the sergeant says:
    No thank you, madam.
Pause.
    Have a good night.

Father settles behind the wheel, belt still off, limp
from shame, tense from anger—a riddle.
We know, once drawn, it must taste blood.
Mother's face sets in a mask,
antivenom for the blacksnake,
balm for the fire of its bite.

LITANY

And that man whose house you sheltered in.
A man with children your age.
A man who loved you for some light invisible to our father.
A man who offered to apprentice you to a merchant's life—
whose gold watch and pen you stole.
Who forgave you, let you keep the trinkets.
A man who brought you home on the motorcycle
you leapt from at full speed, a mile from home,
choosing death over Father's violent embrace.
A man who scrambled down an embankment at night
with me to find you, unharmed in a tangle of bushes.
A man who took Father's slap of shame to his face
with equanimity when he offered money for your freedom
or, the very least, that you be forgiven.
I think of that man sometimes, Brother.
Do you remember his name?

Zealot

Our aunt caressed Jesus on the cross,
fingers slowly tracing muscle, sinew,
a sensuality born of her suffering.
She would press her lips to the cold molded plastic
till they split, blood anointing blood.

And when you asked if she would love Jesus
if he were fat and untortured, she beat you.
That same cross, that same forgiveness,
drew blood from you too. Amen.

We can be loved with the keenness of arrows
by our mothers, and still, in the landscapes
of our poetry, our lives are seamed in the stickiness of blood.

Love is a figure of speech, but also a thing real
as a stone baking in the relentless sun.
We walk everywhere with our shadows.
The bond that holds atoms.

But this train riding through a winter's night
is a light I cling to. Before we say that final
farewell, Brother, before that great sadness,
let it be said that I would like to have a heart
like yours that cooks steaming pots of jollof rice
and invites strangers to eat.

Outside, snow, a white expanse broken
by the defiance of a farmhouse.

LEATHER

This Bible is heavy with vengeance.
Not because its pages chart the path
of the wrathful God of a wrathful people.
But because Father beat us
with its tooled leather-bound weight.
This was the genesis of the smoke,
the retaliation of burning psalms.
We wanted to hold Father accountable
but power is a conceit revealing our limits.
What wounds us makes us complicit.

And so we smoked Father's Bible.
Page by torn page folded into the origami
of an adolescent rebellion.
All these pages inhaled,
the holy evocative power of words and we
remained silly children bound by our fears.
Maybe this is the slippage, when we wonder
how God lets it happen. How a man can
delight in a woman's unbridled joy
then rip it to shreds to keep her from having it.

The mind is deceitful above all things.
It will lie to you in the fragility of paper,
rolled and filled with thyme and lit.
I have seen a tropical storm race
across a savannah like stampeding buffalo,
sheets of rain kicking dust and fear into a haze,
seen a white pigeon unable to fly from a cross,
held in perpetual flutter by the slipstream,
a white flag signaling defeat.
In the end, Brother, we are that pigeon

held in pointless flapping
to a parent oblivious of the love we suffer for.
In a dream, I answered a voiceless call from Father,
wondering what seeks conversation with a ghost.
I will write an elegy on a white sheet of paper,
roll it up and ignite it, watch that burnt offering
ascend to him on a ladder of smoke.

CAMEO: AFTERNOON TEA

The pure delight of a child chewing on a stem of sugarcane.
The elegant lift of cattle egrets into a storm-dark sky.
In the market two women haggle over which
of them the man they share truly loves.
Mother and me drinking tea on the veranda.
And Glenn Miller does the "Chattanooga Choo Choo."
And the sunset betrays another day lost
to the futile work of making a man adore her.
I pour tea, stir sugar into the milk and tannin.
She wonders how many
women like her I will break.

The Bend of Tomorrow

for Chiwoniso

A great psalm brews on her face.
A revolution in her eyes, her hands
poised over metal keys ready to pluck
a new dawn, a new song for Zim.

Remember that guitar we saved up for, Brother?
And when we got it, before we could pluck a single note,
Father burned it, to protect us, he said.
And the flames were the hate of a small heart.

But Chiwoniso he would have liked.
When she held the mbira, that half-womb of song,
to her body and leaned into the microphone,
there was only grace.
In the bar she laughed, husky,
a voice well lived-in, well traveled
across the sinewy terrain of a heart
ravaged by love and tenderness.
It's never what I hear in my head, she says,
shaking the locks piled on her crown.
Never the wonder I approach on the inside.

And I think of you, Brother, and our lungs
smoky and seared from running but never arriving.
Then she laughs, easy, says, *Who can know?*
The song of tomorrow lives somewhere
down the river, around a bend we never reach.
Cesária Évora comes on the radio.
A huddle of poets hushed by a voice
from our hearts. *That*, she says,
as the last whispered note dies. *That.*

FATHER

I have practiced this hate for so long it feels right.
It is not that I haven't forgiven you, angel of my Eden.
It is not that the edge of my sword hasn't dulled.
Forgiveness comes easy, forgetting does not.
There is something here shared with many men—
the love of a father caught in his anger and fists.
We are a generation bred in fear and loathing
and a certain quiet discontent. But there was
melted ice cream and sugar ants picked from it.
An entire childhood can come down to one night.
But that was not all, surely? There was also the hand
that caught me as I fell on rain-slick ground.
And that day you heard me tell
a dirty joke and unable to stop yourself
you laughed loudly, wantonly.

Cameo: The Cut

Do you remember when Mother first tried to leave Father?
In that dusty red-soiled town, our old house
leaning into the seminary's rusty barbed-wire fence?
Begged him to let her go?
We hid behind the torn curtain of the room.
Father smiled. Cruel. Said: *I'm not done with you.*
If you leave I'll have you deported.
You whispered, *Of course she can't leave us.*
No woman can leave five children like a wayward past.
No road can hold that journey. There was a night
I washed her feet, towel dabbing blood
from the cut that opened every day
like a flower, compelled by the crack in the heel
of her wooden clogs, a straight line.
Why do you wear these if they hurt you, I asked.
How can I tell you that this wound is all that
keeps me from killing your father, she replied.
And even in this I learned that hate begets hate,
but sometimes limned by love. Amen.

What Is Traveled, What Is Fragile

When you tear paper, you tear skin, rip a bleat
from a throat that sings. Words
can fail but not sound,
the universe was made from this.
I've never liked snakes yet here I am
winding up this mountainside in a train.
If I must pray, I must slither through
the underbrush, confess fire like the reptile
that carried it in its primordial mouth.
Say *amen*. The first lie they tell in America
is the lie of immigrants. The truth
is America is a nation of refugees
of trauma, displacement, and fanatical hope.
When we say *immigrant*, we mean
I left home but I have nowhere to arrive to.
When they say *immigrant* they mean
an anxiety that leads to murder, erasure—
of indigenous, black, brown, and other bodies stamped
into bedrock, into foundation, into sacrifice, deleted.
Grief is the beast we must all ride,
for the sublime yields only after the grotesque
has been traveled with grace: a living.
Flower cannot precede root.
And when we came upon that rot in the woods,
Brother, body slowly sinking into earth and mulch,
you poked its chest and it burst
into a kaleidoscope of butterflies—
A swarm of color, each one sorrow released,
each one radiance in the dark forest of the self.
In Japan, there is a fable: a koi fish that can
swim up a waterfall becomes a dragon.

How to Kill Your Father

Shaving in that early morning light,
scraping skin thick with sacrifice,
hardened to leather. He left us
standing in the door, blade sounding on rock,
sounding with what he stripped from himself,
with what he would strip from us.
The ritual speech preceded the beating—
a marinade to sweeten violence to love.
A song of *No, no, no* rose to a raspy whisper—
I pushed his face hard into the mirror, his reflection
breaking into a field of shards—blood, glass, razor,
and bellow. And the wan light turned it
from Oedipal to murder—how he howled
and nothing would be the same again.
What I took from him left him diminished
as Lucifer left God. In that light, in that broken mirror,
the face looking back at me broke me.
They say a father should never bury a son,
but they don't tell you a father can never cower
before his son. I had killed my father.
And I was sorry for it, forever sorry for it.

There Are Always Bodies in the Swamp

after Al-Saddiq Al-Raddi

I think silence is our first breach as men, a thread
stitching our jaws closed like the dead.
If we are blessed, we snag an edge and unravel
in language and desire. If we voyage, Brother,
and we must, what is beyond impulse? There is
something like avoidance here, the fear of meaning,
a cartography trod in poems, a pilgrimage in song.
In this train car, open windows and sunlight.
I tap a boiled egg on the window ledge, peel and eat.
Shells patterned in a salted and sharp light.
Walcott in my lap reads: *Slowly my body grows
a single sound, slowly I become a bell.*

Terminus

The true epiphany is that beauty happens
whether we seek it or not.
A boy may become entranced by his shadow,
with the dark, with the incessant. Maybe
we carry death with us. It sits behind the eyes
like a shadow on a lake. Sorrow comes to us
like this at the edge of a sea: an immensity.
I chase my brother across continents, devoutly
following in his footsteps trying to find
the one who cannot be found, the lost boy
who haunts me, almost as if he said:
I will fashion you from your relentless darkness.
Yes, we walk everywhere with our shadows
the way a voice hovers between song and sob,
peels the lines of poetry from the page.
There is no small measure of pyromania
in this, a self-immolation. Sometimes
we are blessed with the night sky,
a leopard, starred and spotted.

PORTAL

Tea in a heavy cast-iron pot.
Steam and a single bamboo stem.
I wear my father's death like a scar.
I wear my brother's death like a scar.
I wear my mother's death like a scar.
Not a talisman but another kind of medicine.
The danger of begging the dead to return
is that sometimes they do:
like that boy whose mother returned
in her slowly decaying wedding dress.
Outside, the snow is preternaturally white,
and silent. A single bamboo stem,
a cast iron pot, and tea—

REVELATION

Light in the garden lush and green
as sky settles into cloud and dark,
the bottom of a fishbowl,
welcome repetition of water,
veil of green light.
I am holding a pen and thinking
of my brother. I am looking at a photograph—
I am six, he is ten.
I am in a long white long-sleeved shirt
with black bow tie, tucked into
too-tight too-short jeans, and with one hand
I am aiming a water pistol. Behind me
in a loose dashiki, hand on my shoulder,
enigmatic smile, he stands,
the sun a splash on his face, light.
I am still six and he is still ten and everything
we could say to each other.
His body is devouring him silently.
This death is a box too heavy to carry
even as thought. Daily
I make offerings before my shrines,
pray for his deliverance,
which is really me asking for reprieve
from the dark, from the rain, from this light.

INCANTATION

What words can you wrap around
a dying brother, still dying, even now.
A man who has not eaten for a month
sips at water and says, *Even thirst is a gift.*
He asks what other gifts God has given him.
I'm your gift, his daughter says from a corner.
And he smiles and rasps—
You can only unwrap a child once.
The rest is prayer and even more prayer.
You sing softly to him in a language
only the two of you speak and he
snores softly into your palm, breath and blood.

Jordan Is No Mere River

I don't know how to work out this loss with you, O God.
If this is blasphemy, then strike, strike—
A fragrance of jasmine from the plant outside,
my answer. Love is a real thing, real as the embrace
of dirt, real as a flower blooming in darkness.
When that first woman slapped the face of a star
on rock with ochre and depth of blue,
it was rebuke to erasure.
Marley, Hayden, Hughes, Awoonor, Okigbo—
the sainted. Ora pro nobis. Word is flame,
the shaper of resurrection.
Here in the Midwest, winter haunts everything,
even a summer afternoon.

To be raised in a violence masked
as a desperate love. In Nsukka
we had to shake our shoes every morning,
empty out any scorpions nesting
in the fading heat of feet.

The hibiscus by the front door died in my absence,
a bad omen despite the white butterfly
insistent on its labor of sweetness.
The work of witchcraft is easier
than losing ourselves to the fear
we cultivate in the dark anger of our histories:
cemetery held up by a barbed-wire fence,
the dead kept in check with metal thorns.
A place of red dust, whirlwinds and ghosts.
Now death feels familiar as my palm on your brow.

We are citizens of displacement, never
recognized for who we are. Never

from where we travel to. A burned
coffee taste like all the cigarette stubs
ground into the earth outside bars.
But here, in the corner of my hallway,
a browning dwarf palm
tries to hold onto legacy, an ordinary sadness.

WING

Delicate as they are it is not the hollowing
that allows birds' bones to rise, to carry prayer.
This is pact, covenant—love for love,
blood for blood, life for life. For this the world exists.

To bear across, which is to say:
I searched for you with a wracking pain.
Does deity recuse itself from our sorrow?
Is it light that strikes to make the shade?
And then night comes and we are saved from sight.

Everywhere the snow and by a roadside,
a blue phone next to a tilting stop sign.
In the Bible there are
500 verses on prayer, 500 verses on faith,
2,000 verses on money and possessions,
1,214 violent or cruel verses, a liturgical math.
Quran means *that which is read.*

The act not the color, affirmation not blood.
In the dark of a prison cell they sometimes wet a bag
and then force you facedown, and squat on your back,
bag pulled over your head until your lungs burn.
Sometimes they just let your lungs burn out, no questions.
A fire made of air can be a thing of mercy, a thing of beauty.

Like the stalking elegance of white cattle egrets
breaking to a startle, a white cloud lifting.

When your dying brother is no more than a tremolo
a hush between worlds
when he makes no more sense
cannot eat or drink, when
he stretches out a hand

in the middle of the night
to a spirit only he can see
when he moans like it is a lamentation,
he is saying *Thank you, thank you, thank you.*

Fragrance

Sometimes grief is acceptance
that love has always been inadequate.
Sometimes it's just another day
and the light comes in through the window.
And my brother calls about ahunji.
An herb somewhere between thyme and clove,
the smell of hunger and satiation at once.
I think of that endless summer of fragrance—
smoke from burning Bible pages, the smell
of burned rice sticking to the pan
lifted into elegy by the smell of crushed ahunji.
And blood, coppery and hot, leaking
from the cane welts on our bodies.
And I make a joke and he laughs, but
it hurts, and he says *Stop, my ribs*—
But he uses the Igbo, *egara*, a word that
opens and closes like a fish's gills,
life and death pulling and pushing.

Ejima

after David St. John

That way the Yoruba carve the likeness
of a child when its twin dies. Carve a doll
for the soul still journeying
across a vale of light and shade.
Dress it in a tunic of leather, cloth,
beads, and cowries. A new birth, a new child,
carried by the mother and fed
with love and breast milk.
Suckled next to the living—flesh to wood,
blood to grain, spirit to body.
When the soul knows
better how to come and go,
when the spirit is warmed from anger,
slowly, over time, it sits by itself on the shrine,
gathers cobwebs and dust and a gentle neglect.
Until then, my brother, I carry your doll,
a photograph of the child you were,
close to my heart. And when you call
in the dark I answer, calm your soul,
sing it into light. In time,
you will join the album on my ancestral shrine
and gather cobwebs and the dust
from the dust, grow sticky
and fat from palm oil and gin,
wear your gentle neglect with a hush.

SCYTHE

I watched your tense quarrel with death.
Gentle snores broken by a body spasming in pain,
screaming into the darkness, still asleep.
And when I stroked your arm and sang, you opened
your eyes wide, took me in and sighed in recognition.
Nwoke, you said, *man*. Just that word, which is to say,
brother, warrior, protector, heart, soul, harbor.
And I said, *Ikpiripiri*, which is to say, *braveheart,*
grace, fighter, strong, love, brother.
You closed your eyes, fell back into oblivion,
and I thought of the grave,
which is to say, resurrection.
Like your garden and its beds of loam thick
with onions and carrots and plump tomatoes.

I think of Mother's garden, how she coaxed harvest
from the most barren soil, made a love of her life,
made tomatoes sweet and heavy on the vine.
Think of the afternoon, amidst all that lushness,
when she was choking and you doused her in cold water,
forced the breath back into her body.

I stood over you with the ice water,
anointed you with prayer and wet.
You lost this round, succumbed to the scythe.
The hospital bed in the living room is empty
like a regret, the faint whiff of disinfectant and body
holds stubbornly to the mute light of a magnolia-
scented candle. This silence calls for voice.

VIGIL

And when our cousin came for you one night,
near the end, in a dream, in a bus,
you called, voice hollow, and said, *I cannot go.*
And we sat together, an ocean between us, talking
of the scent of billy goats and the chili that smells
like them. A hit to the senses.
Talked about how you can
call back across the void if you need me—
all so you wouldn't get on that bus,
travel on to death. A vigil
of laughter and foolishness, a way
to prepare for when you would be ready.

My brother's jaw slackens in death,
mouth falling open, slides to one side.
A waxwork gone awry, melting.
My niece, the doctor, says they will tie it later,
force the rigor and lock with rope—
or one can just hold it until it sets closed.
And so I sit one more vigil
with the blood of my blood.
My hand cups his slowly cooling chin,
and all the while I am singing him
across the gulf of the ineffable,
loss and darkness slain by a jawbone held gently.
Even in this, intimacy is a loaded place, lonely
as a body turning to spirit, still—
I want to ask if I gave enough tenderness,
gave the light, the wick and the flint, gave
the right answers, gave the right *yes.*

Mbubu

1

It is a tenderness, this way
waves rough the shore—
like love, like a moon so full
the ocean cannot sleep for want of it.
And a woman attends the voice of her lover
in this murmur: water over rock, over sand.

2

On a beach in Nigeria, vines heavy with gourds
sound the loss of kin to a pugnacious sea.
On a beach in Jamaica, the other side of Africa's heart,
gourds grow vascular and full, and a reluctant people
carve a presence, a light that swirls
like the guitar's stutter that calls for home
in every chekem of the lick and step and block and slide—*chaa!*
And a stage like the carved-out shell
of a calabash holding the song.

3

My people say: the riddle of our being is in the calabash.
My people say: as big as the sea is, a calabash can hold it.
My people say: there is no loss a bottle gourd cannot contain.
My people say: love is an unending hymn—
a tie left in the grass by a child's hands,
a knot against tomorrow and the fickle wind.

Mbubu is the name of an Afikpo mask carved from a calabash gourd.

CROSSING

That way the shrill of cicadas traps
a summer evening in the thrall of fear.
And doubt enters and you wonder—
is the question *Where is the light*, or *When?*
A simple story is never easy.
That is an elegance learned hard.
Distant thunder and the rustle of muslin.
What do you seek? Story or lighthouse?
Vision or revelation?
I think I will welcome death the way
skin opens to heat.
A lesson learned from Mother's grace
as she sat in a wheelchair,
watching the spread of her family.
The way she leaned back, hands falling open
in her lap to gather light,
or my brother who stopped midshout,
turned to us, smiled and was gone.

The Familiar Is a Texture We Cannot Trust

A blue flame in this cold night,
held to the tip of a rolled-up psalm,
ignites words to fire, to burn.
You take a deep drag and thyme fills the air,
a fragrant smoke. You exhale slowly,
the white cloud plumes, a cloak for your hands.
Passing it to me you stretch your arm
across pages, across myth and history,
your shadow invisible in this deep
night but present.

I remember the burning words:
The Lord stretched the earth over the ocean.
I inhale the chant, feel the power of a king,
feel the tremor of strings and a boy's voice,

but the promise of that spell is broken
by the wince as you adjust your cane-sore buttocks.

And how is it a man can cross fifty and not have witness?
How can I see an angry man in a parking lot with a knife
and a dark bitter vengeance in his heart
and still be surprised by the boy in him?
How did I marvel at rain and moss
and taste the delight of destroying the wet cement blocks
made by a man who toiled alone
in a blistering-hot field to fill his life with order and hope?

Years later I will hear a psalm
in Keorapetse Kgositsile's voice
and I will carry forever that beautiful husk
of a South African poet's voice in the well of me,
a deep resounding. Words sung right can save us.

The Calculus of Faith

In the end I realize
every human body is a scripture.
The first miracle was a mango,
full and weighty with ripeness.
The second miracle was a sheet of onionskin
paper torn from a King James Bible
filled with oregano and thyme and smoked.
The third miracle was the smooth
turquoise of my mother's fountain pen.
The scrape of it, the insistent pull of its nib
and words, glorious and alive.
My fear is a hole I crawl into,
a hollowed-out log, a curve in a stump.
If you listen, if you listen—
in the book I am reading it is raining.

About the Author

Chris Abani is an acclaimed novelist and poet. His most recent books are *The Secret History of Las Vegas*, *The Face: Cartography of the Void*, and *Sanctificum*. He has received a Guggenheim Fellowship, the PEN/Hemingway Award, an Edgar Award, a USA Artists Fellowship, the PEN Beyond Margins Award, a Prince Claus Award, the Hurston/Wright Legacy Award, and a Lannan Literary Fellowship, among many honors. Born in Nigeria, he is a member of the American Academy of Arts and Sciences and a Board of Trustees Professor of English at Northwestern University. He lives in Chicago.

Lannan Literary Selections

For two decades Lannan Foundation has supported the publication and distribution of exceptional literary works. Copper Canyon Press gratefully acknowledges their support.

LANNAN LITERARY SELECTIONS 2022

Chris Abani, *Smoking the Bible*

Victoria Chang, *The Trees Witness Everything*

Nicholas Goodly, *Black Swim*

Dana Levin, *Now Do You Know Where You Are*

Michael Wasson, *Swallowed Light*

RECENT LANNAN LITERARY SELECTIONS FROM COPPER CANYON PRESS

Mark Bibbins, *13th Balloon*

Sherwin Bitsui, *Dissolve*

Jericho Brown, *The Tradition*

Victoria Chang, *Obit*

Leila Chatti, *Deluge*

Shangyang Fang, *Burying the Mountain*

June Jordan, *The Essential June Jordan*

Laura Kasischke, *Lightning Falls in Love*

Deborah Landau, *Soft Targets*

Rachel McKibbens, *blud*

Philip Metres, *Shrapnel Maps*

Aimee Nezhukumatathil, *Oceanic*

Paisley Rekdal, *Nightingale*

Natalie Scenters-Zapico, *Lima :: Limón*

Natalie Shapero, *Popular Longing*

Frank Stanford, *What About This: Collected Poems of Frank Stanford*

Arthur Sze, *The Glass Constellation: New and Collected Poems*

Fernando Valverde, *America* (translated by Carolyn Forché)

Matthew Zapruder, *Father's Day*

Poetry is vital to language and living. Since 1972, Copper Canyon Press has published extraordinary poetry from around the world to engage the imaginations and intellects of readers, writers, booksellers, librarians, teachers, students, and donors.

COPPER CANYON PRESS WISHES TO EXTEND A SPECIAL THANKS TO THE FOLLOWING SUPPORTERS WHO PROVIDED FUNDING DURING THE COVID-19 PANDEMIC:

4Culture
Academy of American Poets (Literary Relief Fund)
City of Seattle Office of Arts & Culture
Community of Literary Magazines and Presses (Literary Relief Fund)
Economic Development Council of Jefferson County
National Book Foundation (Literary Relief Fund)
Poetry Foundation
U.S. Department of the Treasury Payroll Protection Program

WE ARE GRATEFUL FOR THE MAJOR SUPPORT PROVIDED BY:

academy of american poets

THE PAUL G. ALLEN FAMILY FOUNDATION

amazon literary partnership

CULTURE

the point
envision·enact·evolve

Lannan

ART WORKS.
National Endowment for the Arts
arts.gov

A&
OFFICE OF ARTS & CULTURE
SEATTLE

WASHINGTON STATE ARTS COMMISSION

The Witter Bynner Foundation for Poetry

TO LEARN MORE ABOUT UNDERWRITING
COPPER CANYON PRESS TITLES,
PLEASE CALL 360-385-4925 EXT. 103

WE ARE GRATEFUL FOR THE MAJOR SUPPORT PROVIDED BY:

Richard Andrews

Anonymous (3)

Jill Baker and Jeffrey Bishop

Anne and Geoffrey Barker

In honor of Ida Bauer, Betsy
  Gifford, and Beverly Sachar

Donna Bellew

Matthew Bellew

Sarah Bird

Will Blythe

John Branch

Diana Broze

John R. Cahill

Sarah Cavanaugh

Stephanie Ellis-Smith and
  Douglas Smith

Austin Evans

Saramel Evans

Mimi Gardner Gates

Gull Industries Inc. on behalf of
  William True

The Trust of Warren A. Gummow

William R. Hearst III

Carolyn and Robert Hedin

David and Jane Hibbard

Bruce Kahn

Phil Kovacevich and Eric Wechsler

Lakeside Industries Inc. on behalf
  of Jeanne Marie Lee

Maureen Lee and Mark Busto

Peter Lewis and Johnna Turiano

Ellie Mathews and Carl Youngmann
  as The North Press

Larry Mawby and Lois Bahle

Hank and Liesel Meijer

Jack Nicholson

Gregg Orr

Petunia Charitable Fund and
  adviser Elizabeth Hebert

Suzanne Rapp and Mark Hamilton

Adam and Lynn Rauch

Emily and Dan Raymond

Joseph C. Roberts

Jill and Bill Ruckelshaus

Cynthia Sears

Kim and Jeff Seely

Joan F. Woods

Barbara and Charles Wright

In honor of C.D. Wright,
  from Forrest Gander

Caleb Young as C. Young Creative

The dedicated interns and
  faithful volunteers of
  Copper Canyon Press

The Chinese character for poetry is made up
of two parts: "word" and "temple."
It also serves as pressmark for
Copper Canyon Press.

This book is set in Janson Text LT Pro
Book design by Gopa & Ted2, Inc.
Printed on archival-quality paper.